Recipes by Wm. A. Pizzico,
Gina Marie Corporation

Modern Publishing
A Division of Unisystems, Inc.
New York, New York 10022

Printed in Canada

INTRODUCTION

Convenient Cooking™ is just what the modern cook-ordered for quick, easy and delicious food.

Whether you are preparing a simple meal for one, an intimate dinner for two, or a banquet for family or friends, the Convenient Cooking™ series will take the work out of planning and preparing your menus, enabling you to enjoy the occasion and the food!

Eight exciting titles provide a convenient recipe center of easy-to-handle, easy-to-read books for every cooking need: meats and ground meats; seafood; chicken and poultry; soups, salads and sauces; omelettes, casseroles and vegetables; microwave meals; desserts; and Cajun food.

Whether you are a beginning cook, or a seasoned food preparer, you will delight in choosing from the range of basic, traditional fare to exotic meals that this series has to offer.

Welcome to the enjoyable and delicious world of Convenient Cooking.™

CHEDDAR AND BACON OMELETTE

Ingredients:
1 tablespoon butter or
  margarine
4 eggs, beaten
1/4 cup milk
Salt to taste
4 strips bacon, cooked
  crisp, drained
1/2 cup Cheddar
  cheese, shredded

Directions:
Melt butter or margarine in skillet. Spread butter around. Mix eggs, milk and salt in a bowl. Pour into the skillet and cook 5 minutes. Arrange bacon on half of the omelette. Fold over. Sprinkle with cheese. Cover until cheese melts, about 1 more minute.

Serves: 1

HAM AND SWISS PLUS OMELETTE

Ingredients:
2 tablespoons butter or
  margarine
3 eggs, beaten
2 tablespoons milk
1/4 cup ham, cooked
  and chopped fine
2 broccoli flowerettes,
  cooked and separated
3 slices Swiss cheese

Directions:
Heat butter or margarine over medium-high heat. Mix eggs and milk. Pour into pan. When omelette is set on bottom, cover 1 minute. Remove cover and add ham, broccoli and cheese to one side of omelette. Fold other side over top. Reduce heat and cover 1 minute or until cheese melts.

Serves: 1

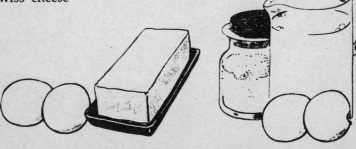

QUICHE PIE

Ingredients:
2 slices Swiss cheese
1 9-inch pie shell, unbaked
1/2 cup spinach, chopped
1/2 cup mushrooms, sliced
1 cup ham, chopped
3 eggs, beaten
1/4 cup Cheddar cheese, shredded
1 cup milk
2 teaspoons flour
1/2 teaspoon salt

Directions:
Place Swiss cheese on bottom of pie shell. Sprinkle spinach, mushrooms and ham over top. Combine eggs, cheese, milk, flour and salt. Pour into pie shell. Bake at 350°F for 40 to 45 minutes.

Serves: 6 to 8

SPINACH AND MUSHROOM OMELETTE

Ingredients:
1 tablespoon butter or margarine
3 eggs, beaten
1/4 cup milk
1/4 cup mushrooms, canned
1/4 cup spinach, cooked and drained

Directions:
Melt butter or margarine in hot non-stick skillet. Briskly stir milk and eggs together. Pour into heated pan. Allow to cook for 2 minutes or until bottom of mixture sets, but is not browned. Cover with lid 1 minute to allow top to set. Uncover. On 1/2 of omelette add mushrooms and spinach. Fold empty side of omelette over mixture side. Cover again and reduce heat to medium-low. Cook 1 minute or until heated through.

Serves: 1

SWISS SOUFFLE

Ingredients:

2 eggs
2/3 cup thick cream
1/2 cup Swiss cheese, diced
1/2 cup American cheese, grated
1/2 cup Parmesan cheese, grated
Salt and pepper to taste
1/4 teaspoon cayenne
1/4 teaspoon nutmeg

Directions:

Combine eggs and cream. Beat slightly. Add cheese, salt, pepper, cayenne and nutmeg. Stir. Pour into souffle dish until 2/3 full. Place into pre-heated 450°F oven for 15 minutes.

Serves: 4

STUFFED ZUCCHINI

Ingredients:
6 to 8 small zucchini
1 cup bread crumbs
1/2 cup grated
  Parmesan cheese
1 teaspoon minced
  onion
2 eggs, slightly beaten
2 tablespoons salad oil
1/4 teaspoon thyme
1/4 teaspoon salt
Garlic salt to taste

Directions:
Trim ends off zucchini. Parboil in boiling salted water 15 minutes and drain. When cool, cut zucchini in half lengthwise. Scoop out insides and reserve. Drain reserved pulp thoroughly. Mix with bread crumbs, 1/4 cup of grated Parmesan, onion, eggs, oil and seasonings. Pile mixture into squash shells. Arrange in a slightly greased casserole dish. Sprinkle with remaining Parmesan. Bake at 350°F for 30 minutes.

Serves: 6

BEEFY TOMATO CASSEROLE

Ingredients:
1/2 pound ground beef
1 onion, chopped
1 green pepper,
  chopped
1 1/2 cups potatoes,
  peeled
Salt to taste
Water
2 cups tomatoes,
  undrained
1/2 cup grated cheese
4 rolls

Directions:
Brown ground beef, onion and green pepper in frying pan. Drain. Place in bottom of casserole dish. Dice potatoes into small cubes. Parboil enough salted water to just cover potatoes. Drain. Layer over ground beef mixture. Pour tomatoes over top. Sprinkle with cheese. Place in a 350°F oven for 20 minutes or until potatoes are tender. Serve with heated rolls.

Serves: 2 to 4

BACON AND POTATO CASSEROLE

Ingredients:

6 potatoes, boiled in
  salt water
4 slices bacon, cooked
  crisp
1/2 cup chopped sweet
  onion
3 tablespoons butter
1 tablespoon flour
1 1/2 cup cream
Salt and pepper to taste

Directions:

Cut boiled potatoes into cubes. Place in casserole dish. Keep warm in a 200°F oven. Crumble bacon, melt butter in skillet and add bacon and onion. Cook over low heat. Mix flour and cream, stir till smooth and pour into dish. Bring to a slow boil. Add bacon and butter and onion. Add salt and pepper to taste. Pour over casserole dish and bake at 350°F for 20 minutes.

Serves: 6 to 8

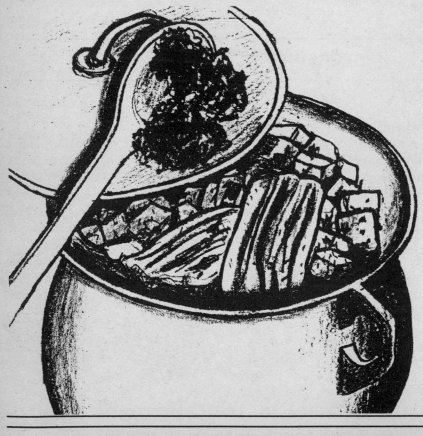

ZUCCHINI AND CHEESE FRITTATA

Ingredients:
1 large tomato
4 tablespoons butter or
  margarine
1 small zucchini,
  unpeeled, sliced 1/4
  inch thick
8 eggs
Salt and pepper to taste
1/2 cup Parmesan
  cheese, grated

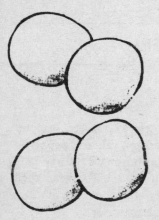

Directions:
Place tomato into very hot water for 1 minute. Remove and peel away skin. Break tomato into tiny pieces, removing seeds. Set aside. Melt 2 tablespoons butter or margarine in a 10-inch skillet. Place zucchini into pan and sauté 2 minutes on each side. Add tomato pieces and simmer until zucchini is just tender. Combine eggs with salt and pepper. Mix well and pour into pan. Cook over medium heat until eggs are set. Sprinkle with cheese. Place pan into preheated broiler 1 minute or until top browns lightly. Let stand a minute before slicing into wedges. *Options:* Cooked and chopped broccoli, green pepper or spinach are also excellent vegetable choices. Add cooked, chopped leftover meats for a hearty meal. Instead of placing frittata in broiler, keep pan on burner. Reduce heat to low and cover. Top will not brown but will set nicely.

Serves: 8

BROCCOLI WITH WILD RICE CASSEROLE

Ingredients:
2 cups wild rice, steamed
3/4 pounds of broccoli flowerettes, parboiled
1 tablespoon butter
1 stalk celery, chopped
1 cup cream of chicken soup
1 cup Cheddar cheese soup
1/2 cup mushrooms

Directions:
Sauté celery in butter for 5 minutes or until tender. In bowl add celery and remaining ingredients except 5 broccoli flowerettes. Mix well and pour into buttered baking dish. Arrange 5 broccoli pieces over top of casserole. Bake for 30 minutes at 350°F oven.

Serves: 6 to 8

CASSEROLE OF BEEF

Ingredients:
4 cups cooked beef cubes
2 cups beef gravy
1/2 cup celery, chopped
1/2 cup carrots, chopped
1 onion, sliced thin
1 cup tomatoes
1 teaspoon non-dairy cream
Salt and pepper to taste
1 cup mushrooms
1 cup potatoes, peeled, cubed, and parboiled for 10 minutes

Directions:
Place beef, gravy, celery, carrots, onions, tomatoes, non-dairy cream, salt and pepper in casserole dish and mix thoroughly. Cover and cook for 1 hour in a 350°F oven. Add remaining ingredients and cook 30 minutes more, until potatoes are tender.

Serves: 8

CHICKEN-RICE CASSEROLE

Ingredients:
1/4 cup margarine or butter
1/3 cup flour
1 1/2 teaspoons salt
1 cup chicken broth
1/4 teaspoon parsley
1 1/2 cup milk
1 1/2 cups cooked white rice or wild rice
2 cups cut-up cooked chicken or turkey
1 (4 ounce) can mushroom stems and pieces, drained
1/3 cup chopped green pepper
2 tablespoons chopped pimento
1/4 cup slivered almonds

Directions:
Heat margarine in 2-quart saucepan until melted. Blend in flour, salt and parsley. Cook over low heat, stirring constantly, until bubbly; remove from heat. Stir in broth and milk. Heat to boiling, stirring constantly. Boil and stir 1 minute. Stir in remaining ingredients. Pour into ungreased 2-quart casserole or oblong baking dish 10 x 6 x 1 1/2 inches. Cook uncovered in 350°F oven until bubbly, 40 to 45 minutes.

Serves: 6

CHICKEN WITH SOUR CREAM CASSEROLE

Ingredients:
1 1/2 pounds chicken, cooked and cubed
1 1/2 tablespoons butter
1 small onion, chopped
1/2 pound mushrooms, sliced and drained
1 tablespoon flour
2/3 cup chicken broth
Salt and pepper to taste
1/2 cup sour cream

Directions:
Preheat oven to 300°F. In a skillet, sauté onion until tender. Add remaining ingredients except sour cream to buttered baking dish. Bake 40 minutes. Stir in sour cream and heat through.

Serves: 4

CUBED LAMB CASSEROLE

Ingredients:
2 pounds lamb, cubed
Salt and pepper to taste
3/4 cup carrots, cut
    into 1-inch strips,
    parboiled
1 cup mashed potatoes
12 small onions, boiled
1 cup green beans,
    cooked
1 teaspoon non-dairy
    cream
2 cups beef gravy

Directions:
Put lamb in skillet. Quickly brown 4 minutes over medium-high heat. Season with salt and pepper. Place in casserole dish and bake 20 minutes in a 375°F oven. Add carrots, potatoes, gravy, salt and pepper. Cook until potatoes are soft. Add onions, beans and non-dairy cream. Spoon all over top and cook 15 minutes more.

Serves: 6

DEVILED HAM CASSEROLE

Ingredients:
1 cup ground ham,
    cooked
2 tablespoons chilli
    sauce
2 teaspoons prepared
    mustard
1 teaspoon minced
    onion
1 teaspoon non-dairy
    cream
1 teaspoon horseradish
2 slices bread
2 tablespoons butter
1/4 cup Cheddar
    cheese, grated
3 eggs, beaten
2 cups milk
Salt and pepper to taste

Directions:
Combine ham, chilli sauce, mustard, onion, non-dairy cream and horseradish. Spread between 2 bread slices. Cut into cubes. Butter a casserole dish and layer cubes and then Cheddar cheese. In a bowl mix eggs, salt, pepper and milk. Pour over the top of casserole. Bake in a 350°F oven for 1 1/4 hours.

Serves: 2

FRESH CORNED BEEF CASSEROLE

Ingredients:

3/4 pounds fresh corned beef, diced

2 cups rice, cooked

1 8-ounce can sauerkraut, rinsed and drained

1 cup Swiss cheese, shredded

1/2 cup mayonnaise

3 tablespoons prepared mustard

Pepper to taste

1 large tomato, sliced

1/2 cup bread crumbs

2 tablespoons relish

Directions:

Combine rice, sauerkraut, corned beef, and 1/2 cup Swiss cheese (save other 1/2 for topping). Blend mayonnaise, relish, mustard and pepper. Stir into rice mixture. Place into shallow 2 - quart casserole dish. Arrange tomato slices on top. Sprinkle with remaining cheese. Top with bread crumbs. Place in a preheated 350°F oven for about 30 minutes or until hot and bubbly.

Serves: 4 to 6

FRUITED HAM AND SWEET POTATO CASSEROLE

Ingredients:

4 sweet potatoes, peeled and cut thin

1 pound ham, cooked and sliced into 1-inch pieces

4 apples peeled, sliced thick

1/4 cup butter

1/4 cup brown sugar

1/4 cup raisins

Directions:

Place 1/2 of potatoes into greased baking dish. Layer ham pieces over top. Layer apples over ham. Melt butter and brown sugar in saucepan. Add raisins and remaining ingredients to casserole. Pour remaining sauce in dish and bake 45 minutes in a 325°F oven.

Serves: 4 to 6

GREEN BEANS AND MUSHROOM CASSEROLE

Ingredients:
1 10-ounce package
   green beans cooked
   and drained
1 10-ounce package
   yellow beans cooked
   and drained
1 4-ounce can
   mushroom caps,
   drained
1 small onion, chopped
   and sautéed
1/4 cup water
1 10 1/2-ounce can
   cream of mushroom
   soup
1/2 cup French fried
   onion pieces

Directions:
Mix beans, onions, soup and mushrooms and water and pour into buttered casserole dish. Top with onion pieces and bake at 350°F for 25 minutes.

Serves: 4

GROUND HAM AND NOODLE CASSEROLE

Ingredients:
1 pound flat noodles,
   cooked 3/4 done
1 pound ground ham,
   cooked
2 tablespoons water
1 scallion, minced
1/4 cup parsley
4 eggs
2/3 cups light cream
1/4 cup Parmesan
   cheese
1/4 pound butter
1/2 cup bread crumbs
Salt and pepper to taste

Directions:
Combine ham, bread crumbs, water, scallions, parsley and salt and pepper to taste. Alternate noodles and ham mixture in baking dish. Mix eggs, cream, cheese and butter. Pour over baking dish mixture and cook 45 minutes at 350°F.

Serves: 8

HEARTY AMERICAN OMELETTE

Ingredients:

1/2 can tuna, packed in water

1 tablespoon mayonnaise

1 tablespoon butter or margarine

4 eggs, beaten

1/4 cup milk

Salt to taste

3 strips bacon, cooked crisp

4 tomato slices

3 slices American cheese

Directions:

Mix tuna with mayonnaise and set aside. Melt butter or margarine in skillet. Combine eggs, milk and salt in a bowl. Mix well. Pour into skillet. Cook 5 minutes or until bottom is firm. If egg is very loose on top, lift edges with spatula to allow egg to run under omelette. Cook 1 more minute. Spoon tuna on half of the omelette. Place bacon over tuna. Fold omelette over. Arrange tomatoes over omelette. Top with cheese. Cover and cook 2 minutes more or until cooked through.

Serves: 1-2

HOT DOG AND SAUERKRAUT CASSEROLE

Ingredients:
1/2 pound sauerkraut, drained
1/2 cup beer, flat
1/4 cup caraway seeds
6 hot dogs, cut into thirds

Directions:
Place all ingredients in casserole dish except hot dogs. Cover and bake 10 minutes in 350°F oven. Arrange hot dogs over top and bake 20 minutes more.

Serves: 6

HONEY HAM AND SWEET POTATOES

Ingredients:
1 pound ham steaks
1 10-ounce can sweet potatoes, drained
3/4 cup orange juice
1/4 cup honey
1/4 cup raisins
1 teaspoon prepared mustard

Directions:
Place ham in large Dutch oven. Over medium-high heat sear 1 minute on each side. Arrange potatoes around ham. Combine orange juice, honey, raisins and mustard. Mix well. Brush over ham and potatoes. Pour remaining mixture over top. Cover and simmer 15 minutes, basting once or twice.

Serves: 4

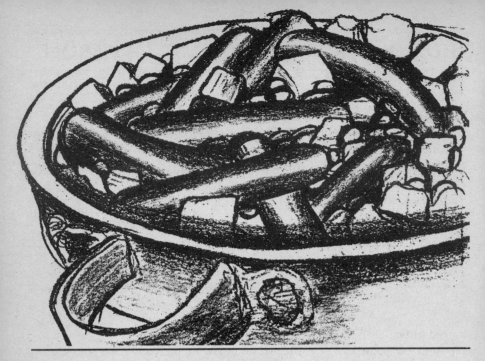

HAWAIIAN FRANKS AND BEANS

Ingredients:

1 (20 ounce) can
  pineapple rings;
  reserve juice
2 tablespoons butter or
  margarine
1 green pepper, cut into
  1-inch squares
1 medium onion, sliced
2 tablespoons soy sauce
2 tablespoons prepared
  mustard
1/3 cup tomato catsup
1/3 cup brown sugar
4 cups pork and beans
1 package frankfurters
Maraschino cherries

Directions:

Cut all except 4 pineapple rings into chunks and set aside. Melt butter or margarine in skillet. Add green pepper, onion and pineapple chunks. Simmer until onion becomes clear. Add reserved juice from pineapple, soy sauce, mustard, catsup and brown sugar. Bring to a boil. Immediately pour into casserole dish. Add beans and stir until mixed thoroughly. Arrange frankfurters and pineapple rings over top. Place cherries in the center of each pineapple ring. Bake in a 325°F oven for 40 minutes.

Serves: 6 to 8

ITALIAN CASSEROLE

Ingredients:

1 1/2 pounds steak,
  thinly sliced
1/2 cup celery, diced
1 small onion, chopped
Salt and pepper to taste
1/2 pound white rice
1 can golden cream of
  mushroom soup
1 cup beef gravy
1/2 cup water
1/4 cup milk
1/2 cup black olives

Directions:

In saucepan, add steak, celery, onion, salt and pepper. Cook till tender. Place in bowl and mix remaining ingredients together. Spread mixture in buttered casserole dish and cover with olives. Bake 350°F for 1 hour.

Serves: 4

LAMB AND EGGPLANT CASSEROLE

Ingredients:

1 eggplant, peeled and
  cut into cubes
Salt to taste
2 tablespoons flour
1 cup Cheddar cheese,
  shredded
1 small green pepper,
  chopped
1 small onion, chopped
2 cups tomato juice
2 cups lamb, diced and
  cooked
1 cup croutons

Directions:

Combine green peppers, onion and salt. Simmer for 10 minutes. Grease a shallow, heatproof baking dish and mix flour and tomato juice till it forms a smooth paste. Stir in vegetables. Simmer over medium heat until thickened; about 3 minutes. Add lamb, vegetables and cheese in a layered fashion then top with croutons. Bake 20 minutes at 350°F.

Serves: 4

LAMB AND VEGETABLE CASSEROLE

Ingredients:
1 (10 ounce) package lima beans, frozen
1 1/2 cups carrots, thinly sliced
1 cup boiling water
1 1/2 pounds ground lamb
1 tablespoon onion, chopped
1 tablespoon cooking oil
1 (19 1/2 ounce) can cream of mushroom soup, condensed
1/3 cup vegetable liquid (liquid reserved from cooking vegetables)
1/2 teaspoon salt
1/4 teaspoon thyme
6 tomatoes, sliced 3/4 inch thick
2 tablespoons Parmesan cheese

Directions:
Add lima beans and carrots to boiling water. Cover and cook until they are tender, about 10 minutes. Remove vegetables from the pan saving liquid, and set aside. Preheat oven to 350°F. Cook ground lamb and onion in cooking oil until lamb is lightly browned and the onion is transparent. Pour off excess fat and add condensed soup, vegetable liquid, vegetables, salt and thyme. Mix well. Pour into a 2-quart casserole dish. Arrange tomato slices on top of mixture. Sprinkle with cheese. Bake at 350°F for 25 to 30 minutes.

Serves: 6

LASAGNA ROLL-UPS

Ingredients:

10 strips of lasagna
    noodles
1/2 pound sausage,
    cooked and crumbled
3 cups spaghetti sauce
1 pound ricotta cheese
1/2 cup grated
    Parmesan cheese plus
    2 tablespoons for top
1 egg, beaten
1 teaspoon oregano

Directions:

Cook lasagna noodles according to instructions on package. Lay noodles flat. On bottom of baking pan pour a third of sauce. Combine cheeses, eggs and oregano. Spread a thin layer on top of each noodle. Roll up jellyroll style, placing seam side down. Place in pan and spoon remaining sauce on top. Bake 20 minutes. Sprinkle 2 tablespoons Parmesan cheese over top and cook 10 minutes more. in a 350°F oven.

Serves: 5 to 10

LUNCHEON CASSEROLE

Ingredients:

1 pound bacon, cooked,
    drained and crumbled
6 eggs, beaten with
    mixer
2 slices bread, cubed
2 cups milk
1 cup Cheddar cheese,
    melted
1 teaspoon dry mustard
1 teaspoon non-dairy
    cream
1 teaspoon salt
5 slices tomato

Directions:

Thoroughly mix all ingredients except tomatoes in a bowl. Flatten into casserole dish. Bake in a 350°F oven for 40 minutes. Place tomatoes over top and bake for 5 minutes more.

Serves: 3

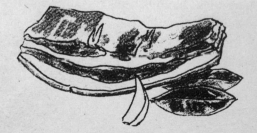

MASHED POTATO CASSEROLE

Ingredients:
4 cups mashed potatoes
1/2 cup butter
1/2 cup light cream
1 onion chopped
Salt and pepper to taste
4 eggs, beaten
1/2 cup fried onion
  rings

Directions:
Sauté onion in butter. Mix remaining ingredients, except onion rings, with mixer for approximately 2 minutes on high speed. Pour into casserole dish. Top with onion rings. Bake 30 minutes in a 325°F oven.

Serves: 4 to 8

MEDITERRANEAN CHUCK STEW

Ingredients:
2 tablespoons salad oil
2 pounds boneless beef,
  cut into 1-inch cubes
1 (28 ounce) can whole
  tomatoes, broken up
1 cup water
2 teaspoons
  Worcestershire sauce
1 eggplant (1 pound)
  unpeeled, cut into
  1-inch cubes
2 medium zucchini, cut
  into 1/2-inch slices
1 1/2 teaspoons salt

Directions:
Heat oil in large saucepan until hot. Add half of beef cubes and brown on all sides. Remove meat with slotted spoon and set aside. Brown remaining beef cubes and drain off drippings. Return all meat to saucepan; add tomatoes, water, salt and Worcestershire sauce. Bring to a boil. Reduce heat and simmer covered, until meat is almost tender, about 1 1/2 hours. Add eggplant; simmer covered, 10 minutes. Add zucchini; simmer covered, until meat and vegetables are tender, about 10 minutes.

Serves: 6

MUSHROOM SOUP CASSEROLE

Ingredients:
2 cups rotini pasta, cooked and drained
1 (7 ounce) can tuna, drained
1 cup cream of mushroom soup, condensed
1 cup milk
1 small can toasted onion rings
1/4 tablespoon bottled steak sauce

Directions:
Pour a layer of pasta on the bottom of a baking dish. Next, sprinkle a layer of tuna. Repeat layers. Mix soup, milk and steak sauce. Add to dish. Sprinkle with onion rings. Bake in a 450°F oven for 20 minutes.

Serves: 3

"NO FUSS" HAM CASSEROLE

Ingredients:
2 cups macaroni
2 eggs, beaten
1/2 cup milk
1 teaspoon prepared mustard
Salt to taste
12 ounces cooked ham, cut into small chunks
1 (8 ounce) can mushrooms; drained
1 small green pepper, chopped fine
1 cup bread, diced
1 cup Cheddar cheese, grated
1/2 cup Swiss cheese, grated

Directions:
Prepare macaroni as directed on package and set aside. Combine eggs, milk, mustard and salt. Beat well. Add macaroni, three-quarters of the ham, and the mushroom caps, green pepper, bread and cheeses. Gently stir until ingredients are coated with egg mixture. Pour into 2-quart baking dish. Arrange remaining ham over top. Place in a 350°F oven for 25 minutes.

Serves: 4 to 6

NOODLE CASSEROLE

Ingredients:
8 eggs
1 cup butter, melted
1 (8 ounce) package cream cheese, room temperature
1 pint sour cream
1 tablespoon chives, finely chopped
1/4 pound small shell noodles, cooked as directed on package
1/4 pound ruffle noodles, cooked as directed on package

Directions:
Mix all ingredients, except noodles, in a bowl. Add noodles and mix. Pour into a 9 x 13 x 1 1/2 inch baking pan. Bake for 20 minutes at 350°F.

Serves: 4

ORIENTAL CHICKEN CASSEROLE

Ingredients:
2 1/2 to 3 pounds boneless chicken or chicken parts
3 eggs
3 tablespoons soy sauce
Flour as needed
1 (10 ounce) package frozen Oriental vegetables
2 cups cooked rice

Directions:
Dip chicken pieces in mixture of eggs and soy sauce then coat with flour. Place the chicken in a shallow baking pan and bake at 350°F approximately 40 minutes or until done. Meanwhile, cook vegetables according to package directions. Combine vegetables and rice in a serving dish, top with chicken, sprinkle with soy sauce and serve. *Helpful Hints:* Coating the chicken with flour keeps the moisture added by the egg and soy sauce from escaping. The result is naturally tender, moist chicken.

Serves: 4 to 6

PORK AND BEAN CASSEROLE

Ingredients:
4 pork steaks
1 (10 ounce) can pork
  and beans
1/2 cup catsup
1/2 cup barbecue sauce
1/4 cup brown sugar
1/4 cup water

Directions:
Brown pork steaks in 375°F oven for about 10 minutes. Mix remaining ingredients. Pour over pork chops, cover and bake in a 325°F oven for 45 minutes.

Serves: 4

PORK STEAK CASSEROLE

Ingredients:
4 pork steaks, 1/2 inch
  thick
1 cup rice, uncooked
1/2 cup mushrooms
1 onion, sliced
Salt and pepper to taste
1 1/2 cups beef stock

Directions:
Arrange pork steaks in baking dish. Brown steaks in a 375°F oven for 10 minutes. Add rice and sprinkle salt and pepper over top. Sprinkle with mushrooms and onion. Pour stock over top. Place in 375°F oven for 30 minutes. Cover with foil. Cook 15 minutes more.

Serves: 4

RICE AND CHEESE COMBO

Ingredients:
1/4 cup butter or margarine
4 cups rice, steamed
1/4 pound Cheddar cheese, shredded
2 teaspoons cayenne pepper
Milk, enough to cover half of the ingredients in baking dish
1/4 cup bread crumbs

Directions:
Coat baking dish with 1 tablespoon butter or margarine. Cover bottom of baking dish with a thin layer of rice. Place small amounts of butter over rice. Sprinkle some Cheddar cheese and cayenne over top. Repeat layers until all ingredients are used up. Add milk. Cover with bread crumbs. Place in 350°F oven for 20 minutes or until cheese melts.

Serves: 4 to 6

RICE-TOMATO-SPINACH CASSEROLE

Ingredients:
1 (1 pound, 4 ounce) can tomatoes
1 (10 ounce) package frozen chopped spinach
Dash garlic salt
Dash pepper
1 teaspoon salt
1 cup water
1 cup quick-cooking rice

Directions:
In an ovenproof 2-quart casserole, combine tomatoes, spinach and seasonings; heat. When hot, add water and bring to a boil. Add rice; lower heat and let steam, covered, 15 minutes or until ready to serve.

Serves: 6

ROAST BEEF AND SPINACH CASSEROLE

Ingredients:
2 cups creamed spinach
1 small onion, minced
1 clove garlic, crushed
8 slices roast beef
1 cup beef gravy

Directions:
Mix spinach, onion and garlic in bowl. Pour into casserole dish. Roll up roast beef slices and place roast beef in dish. Pour gravy over top. Bake in 400°F oven for 30 minutes or until thoroughly heated through.

Serves: 4

SCALLOP CASSEROLE

Ingredients:
1 (12 ounce) package frozen scallops, thawed, or 12 ounces fresh scallops
3/4 cup half-and-half
1 cup dried bread crumbs
1/2 cup butter or margarine, melted
2 teaspoons celery seed
1 teaspoon salt
1/4 teaspoon pepper
1/4 teaspoon garlic salt
Paprika

Directions:
If scallops are large, cut into 1 1/2-inch pieces. Remove any shell particles and wash scallops. Arrange in greased 12 x 7 1/2 x 2 inch oblong baking dish, or a 9 x 9 x 2 inch square pan. Pour about half of the half-and-half on scallops. Mix bread crumbs, margarine, celery seed, salt, pepper and garlic salt; sprinkle over scallops. Top with remaining half-and-half (liquid should come about three-quarters of the way up on scallops). Sprinkle with paprika. Cook, uncovered, in 375°F oven until hot and bubbly, 25 to 30 minutes.

Serves: 5

SAUSAGE CASSEROLE

Ingredients:

1 tablespoon cooking oil

1 pound bulk sausage, peeled

1 cup of potatoes, sliced

1 green pepper, chopped

1 small onion, chopped

5 eggs

1 1/2 cups milk

3/4 teaspoons baking soda

1/2 cup Parmesan cheese, grated

Directions:

Rub bottom of casserole dish with oil. Crumble sausage in dish. Layer potatoes, green peppers and onion on top. Bake 30 minutes in a 350°F oven. Combine eggs, milk, baking soda and cheese in bowl. Beat with fork for 1 minute. Pour over top and reduce heat to 325°F and bake 30 minutes more.

Serves: 4 to 6

SCALLOPED TOMATOES CASSEROLE

Ingredients:
3 tablespoons butter or margarine
1 cup celery, finely chopped
1/2 cup onion, finely chopped
2 tablespoons flour
2 slices bread, toasted
3 1/2 cups tomatoes, peeled and cooked
1 tablespoon sugar
1 teaspoon salt
Dash of pepper
2 teaspoons prepared mustard

Directions:
In 2 tablespoons butter or margarine, sauté celery and onion until just tender. Stir in flour until mixed well. Cover and set aside. Spread toasted bread with remaining butter or margarine and cut into 1/2-inch cubes. Combine bread cubes, tomatoes, sugar, salt, pepper and mustard with celery mixture. Pour combination into casserole or baking dish. Bake at 350°F for 45 minutes. *Options:* Use an extra slice of toasted, buttered bread cut into 1/2 inch cubes to be used as croutons. Sprinkle over top of recipe 20 minutes before cooking time is done.

Serves: 8

SEAFOOD CASSEROLE

Ingredients:
2 tablespoons butter
3/4 pounds halibut, flounder, cod or other seafood, cooked
2 cups prepared marinara sauce
1/4 cup white wine, dry
Salt and pepper to taste
2 cups cooked rice

Directions:
In casserole dish, melt butter. Layer fish and rice. Heat 3 minutes. Pour in sauce and wine, cover and simmer 20 minutes.

Serves: 4 to 6

SPICY OMELETTE

Ingredients:
1/2 cup thick tomato
   sauce
1/4 cup mushrooms
Tabasco sauce to taste
1 tablespoon butter or
   margarine
4 eggs, beaten
1/4 cup milk
Salt to taste
1/4 cup mozzarella
   cheese, shredded

Directions:
Mix sauce, mushrooms and Tabasco in saucepan. Heat while omelette cooks. Melt butter or margarine in large skillet. Combine eggs, milk and salt in a bowl. Mix well. Pour into skillet. Cook 5 minutes or until bottom is firm. If egg is very loose on top, lift edges with spatula to allow egg to run under omelette. Cook 1 more minute. Place cheese over half of omelette. Spoon mushrooms over top. Fold half of omelette without cheese and mushrooms over the top of the cheese. Cook 3 minutes or until done. Remove to platter and pour sauce over top.

Serves: 1

TURKEY CASSEROLE WITH ALMONDS

Ingredients:
2 cups turkey, cooked
1 cup wild rice, cooked
Salt to taste
1 cup yogurt
1 cup milk
1 can cream of
   mushroom soup
1/4 cup almonds,
   slivered
1 tablespoon poultry
   seasoning
1/2 cup bread crumbs
2 tablespoons butter

Directions:
Mix all ingredients except bread crumbs and butter. Mix bread crumbs and butter together. Put turkey mixture into buttered casserole dish and sprinkle top of casserole with bread crumbs. Bake at 350°for 35 minutes.

Serves: 8

TURKEY DIVAN

Ingredients:
1 10-ounce package
  onion rings
2 cups turkey, cut up
  and cooked
2 10-ounce packages
  broccoli
1/2 cup Cheddar
  cheese, shredded
1/2 cup American
  cheese, shredded
1/2 can cream of
  mushroom soup,
  condensed
1 can evaporated milk

Directions:
Prepare onion rings as directed on package and set aside. Place turkey evenly on bottom of baking dish, laying broccoli and cheese over top. Combine soup with milk and pour into baking dish. Cover. Place in 325°F oven for 30 minutes. Remove from oven. Place onion rings over top and return to oven, uncovered for 5 minutes longer.

Serves: 2 to 4

VEAL AND VEGETABLE CASSEROLE

Ingredients:
1 10-ounce package
  lima beans, frozen
1 cup boiling water
1 small onion
1 10 1/2-ounce can
  condensed cream of
  mushroon soup
Salt and pepper to taste
1 1/2 cups carrots,
  sliced thin
1 1/2 cups ground veal
1 tablespoon cooking
  oil
1/3 cup tomato juice
6 tomato slices
2 tablespoons grated
  Parmesan cheese

Directions:
Add beans and carrots to boiled salted water and cook for 15 minutes. Drain. Preheat oven to 350°F. In baking dish, cook veal and onion in oil for 10 minutes, stir and drain. Add soup, juice, vegetables and salt, mix well. Arrange tomatoes over top and sprinkle with cheese. Bake 35 minutes.

Serves: 8

VEGETABLE CASSEROLE

Ingredients:
3 tablespoons butter
1/2 cup green pepper
1/2 cup carrots, cooked
1/2 cup corn, cooked
1/4 cup celery
1 1/2 cups chicken broth
3 tablespoons flour
2 eggs, slightly beaten

Directions:
Melt butter in baking dish. Add green peppers and celery and bake for 5 minutes in 375°F oven. Stir in carrots and corn. Heat broth in saucepan. Stir in flour, stirring until lumps dissolve. Add eggs, and cook over low heat. Stir until thickened, approximately 5 minutes, and then pour over vegetables. Bake for 25 minutes in 350°F oven.

Serves: 3

WELSH RAREBIT CASSEROLE

Ingredients:
7 slices bread
3 tablespoons butter, softened
1 cup Cheddar cheese, grated
2 eggs
1 cup milk
1/2 teaspoon dried mustard
Salt and pepper to taste

Directions:
Butter bread, then cut 2 slices into half-triangle shapes. Set aside. Cut remaining bread into 1-inch cubes. Butter baking dish and add bread cubes. Sprinkle cheese over top. With mixer on high speed, beat eggs, mustard and milk. Pour over cheese. Arrange triangles around mixture with center points facing up. Place in 350°F oven for 25 minutes. Serve immediately.

Serves: 4

ZUCCHINI AND TOMATO CASSEROLE

Ingredients:
1 onion chopped
1/4 cup butter
2 to 3 small zucchini
   sliced
3 1/2 cups tomatoes,
   drained
Salt and pepper to taste
1/4 cup bread crumbs

Directions:
Cook onion and zucchini in butter until lightly browned, approximately 5 minutes. Add tomatoes and salt and pepper to taste. Mix well and pour into casserole dish. Top with bread crumbs and bake in 350°F oven for 30 minutes.

Serves: 6

BAKED POTATOES AU GRATIN

Ingredients:
2 cups cooked potatoes, boiled
1 1/2 cups heavy cream
1 tablespoon butter or margarine
3/4 cups Cheddar cheese, shredded fine

Directions:
In bowl, combine potatoes and heavy cream. Stir until potatoes are well coated. Coat baking dish with butter or margarine. Place 1/3 of potato mixture in dish. Sprinkle with 1/3 of grated cheese. Continue alternating 1/3 of each. Place in 325°F oven for 20 minutes or until thoroughly heated and cheese melts.

Serves: 6

BOILED CABBAGE

Ingredients:
1 2-pound head of cabbage, outer leaves removed, stem trimmed
1 1/2 quarts water
Salt and pepper to taste

Directions:
Cut cabbage through stem in quarters. Place in water, bring to boil and reduce heat. Add salt and pepper. Cover and simmer 20 minutes or until tender, but not soft. *Options:* Sprinkle with vinegar or grated cheese. Spoon tomato sauce over top and sprinkle with Parmesan cheese. Serve with butter or margarine. Add ham or bacon while boiling for added flavor. *Helpful Hints:* Dividing through stem prevents cabbage from falling apart while cooking. Therefore you will have neat portions to serve.

Serves: 4

BRAISED ENDIVE

Ingredients:
4 cups water
1/2 pound endive,
  bottom core removed
Salt to taste
1/4 cup butter or
  margarine
2 tablespoons Parmesan
  cheese

Directions:
Place water, endive and salt in large pot. Bring to boil, reduce heat and cover. Simmer 10 minutes, stirring occasionally. Drain well. Add butter or margarine and cheese. Simmer 4 minutes more. *Options:* Sprinkle with vinegar. Stir in mushrooms or kidney beans. *Helpful Hints:* Delicious served with meat poultry or seafood.

Serves: 2 to 4

BUTTER SPINACH RING

Ingredients:
1 pound spinach
Water, enough to cover
  spinach halfway
Salt to taste
1/3 cup butter

Directions:
Place spinach in water. Bring to boil, add salt and reduce heat. Cover and simmer 15 minutes or until tender, but not soft. Drain well. Chop fine, add butter and stir. Press evenly in ring mold. Place platter over top mold and invert together. Gently lift ring mold away from spinach. *Options:* Add finely chopped mushrooms, walnuts or slivered almonds. Add 1/2 cup cooked rice to spinach after draining. Grated cheese adds a delicious touch when mixed with spinach. Margarine can be used in place of butter. Try other shaped molds for a change of pace. *Helpful Hints:* Ring can be served alone or filled with meat, poultry or seafood mixture. An attractive addition to any dinner table.

Serves: 6

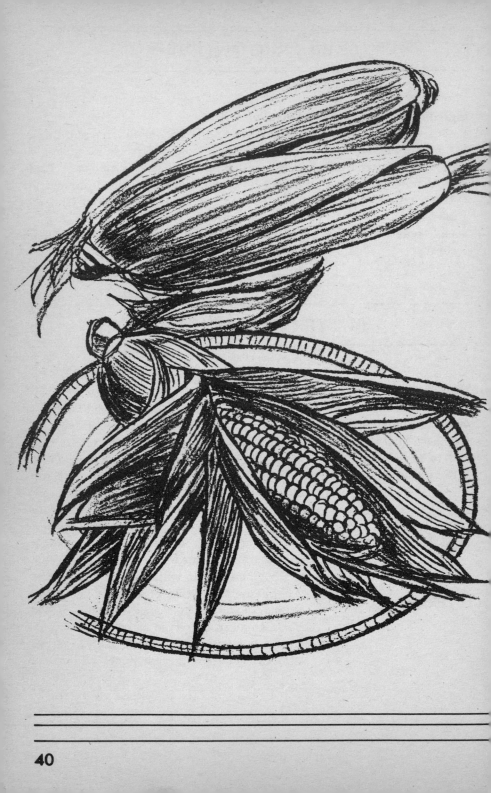

BUTTERY CORN ON THE COB

Ingredients:
2 quarts water
4 ears of corn, husked
2 teaspoons salt
2 tablespoons butter or
   margarine

Directions:
Boil water. Add corn and salt. Cook over medium heat for 10 minutes or until tender. Remove to platter. Brush with butter and season to taste.

Serves: 4

CARROT MOLD

Ingredients:
2 cups cooked carrots,
   grated fine
1 1/2 cups Parmesan
   cheese, grated
2 eggs, beaten
1 cup bread crumbs
1 cup milk
2 tablespoons butter or
   margarine

Directions:
Combine carrots, cheese, eggs, bread crumbs and milk. Mix well. Pour into baking dish or ring mold, lightly coated with butter or margarine. Bake 1 hour at 350°F. *Options:* Spinach also works well in this recipe in place of carrots. *Helpful Hints:* To loosen recipe from mold, set mold into pan of hot water almost to top, for 30 seconds.

Serves: 6

CANDIED SWEET POTATOES

Ingredients:
1 large can sweet
   potatoes, drained
1/2 cup brown sugar
2 tablespoons butter or
   margarine, melted
1 teaspoon corn syrup
Salt and pepper to taste

Directions:
Line bottom of baking pan with foil. Arrange potatoes on foil. Combine sugar, butter, syrup, salt and pepper in bowl. Mix well. Pour over potatoes. Place pan in a preheated broiler for 7 minutes or until thoroughly heated. Baste with brown sugar mixture as potatoes broil. Carefully remove potatoes from pan and pour glaze over top.

Serves: 4

CABBAGE WITH TOMATO SAUCE

Ingredients:

1 small head cabbage
1 1/2 cups tomato
    sauce
2 tablespoons Parmesan
    cheese, grated

Directions:

Cut cabbage into quarters and then into eighths, cutting away end of core. Arrange cabbage wedges in large skillet. Pour sauce over top and sprinkle with cheese. Cover and simmer, basting with sauce occasionally. Simmer 30 minutes or until cabbage is tender but not wilted. *Options:* Add sliced mushrooms before simmering. *Helpful Hints:* If sauce should thicken too much, add water 1 tablespoon at a time till desired consistency. Cabbage can be removed from pan and served in neat wedges if allowed to remain a little firm.

Serves: 4 to 6

CARROTS UNDER A CLOUD

Ingredients:

3 cups mashed potatoes,
    seasoned, hot
1 pound carrots, scraped
    and sliced
4 cups boiling water
Salt to taste
1 egg, beaten
3 tablespoons butter or
    margarine, softened
1 clove garlic, minced
    fine
2 tablespoons grated
    Parmesan cheese

Directions:

Set potatoes aside. Add carrots to boiling water. Add salt and cook over medium heat for 20 minutes or until very tender. Drain. In bowl mash carrots with fork until lumps disappear. Mix in egg, butter and garlic. Flatten loosely on bottom of baking dish. Spoon potatoes over top. Sprinkle with cheese and bake in a 350°F oven for 30 minutes.

Serves: 4-6

CHEDDAR CAULIFLOWER

Ingredients:
2 quarts water
Salt to taste
1 head cauliflower
flowerettes, separated
3/4 cup Cheddar cheese
spread
1/4 cup Parmesan
cheese, grated
1/4 cup of milk
2 tablespoons
Worcestershire sauce

Directions:
Bring water and salt to boil. Add cauliflower. Bring water to boil again. Reduce heat to medium-low and cover. Simmer 15 minutes. Meanwhile add cheese, milk and sauce in saucepan. Stir over medium heat until smooth. Drain cauliflower and arrange on platter. Pour hot sauce over top.

Serves: 4

CORN FRITTERS

Ingredients:
1 cup fresh or frozen
corn
1 egg, beaten
3/4 cup flour
1/2 teaspoon baking
powder
1/2 teaspoon salt
1/4 cup cooking oil
1/4 cup powdered sugar

Directions:
Combine corn and egg in bowl. Slowly add flour, baking powder and salt. Mix well. Heat oil in pan. By spoonful, place batter in hot oil. Fry 3 minutes on each side or until golden brown. Drain. Sprinkle with powdered sugar.

Serves: 6

CREAMED PEAS AND ONIONS

Ingredients:
1 (16 ounce) can peas, undrained
1/2 cup tiny, whole onions, cooked
1/2 cup non-dairy cream

Directions:
Pour undrained peas and onions into saucepan and heat through. Drain. Stir in non-dairy cream. Cover and simmer until sauce is hot and bubbly, about 4 minutes. *Options:* Use fresh or frozen peas, if desired.

Serves: 4

DEEP-FRIED CAULIFLOWER

Ingredients:
1 head cauliflower
1 egg, beaten
1 1/2 cups bread crumbs, seasoned
4 cups cooking oil
Salt and pepper to taste

Directions:
Separate cauliflower into flowerettes. Dip in egg on all sides, then coat with bread crumbs. Heat cooking oil in deep fryer set at 370°F. Add cauliflower 2 or 3 pieces at a time. Fry until golden brown. Place on paper towels to drain. Season with salt and pepper. *Options:* Pan fry in 1 to 2 inches of oil. Try broccoli for an equally delicious treat. Sprinkle with vinegar and oil dressing. *Helpful Hints:* Serve as a side dish, or as an appetizer. Buy cauliflower that is firm and white without discoloring. If brown spots appear, scraping with a knife will remove them easily.

Serves: 4

DILL BEANS AND CARROTS

Ingredients:
3/4 cups water
Salt to taste
1 teaspoon sugar
1/2 teaspoon dill seed
1/2 pound green beans, ends removed
1/2 pound carrots, sliced
1/4 cup creamy Italian dressing, bottled

Directions:
Place water, salt, sugar and dill in saucepan. Bring to boil. Snap beans in 1-inch pieces. Place in boiling water. Simmer over medium-low heat for 7 minutes. Add carrots. Continue cooking 10 minutes more so that water is almost evaporated. Drain. Remove to platter and pour dressing over top. Toss lightly.

Serves: 6

EGGPLANT PARMESAN

Ingredients:
1 small eggplant peeled, sliced
2 eggs, beaten
1 cup bread crumbs, seasoned
3 tablespoons cooking oil
3/4 cups mozzarella cheese, shredded
2 cups tomato sauce

Directions:
Dip eggplant in egg, then coat with bread crumbs. Heat oil in large skillet. Place eggplant in oil. Fry 5 minutes on each side or until golden brown. Drain, then arrange in long baking pan. Sprinkle mozzarella cheese over eggplant. Pour sauce over top. Place in a 350°F oven for 30 minutes.

Serves: 6 to 8

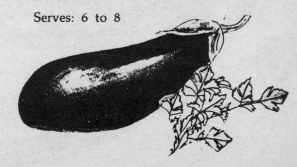

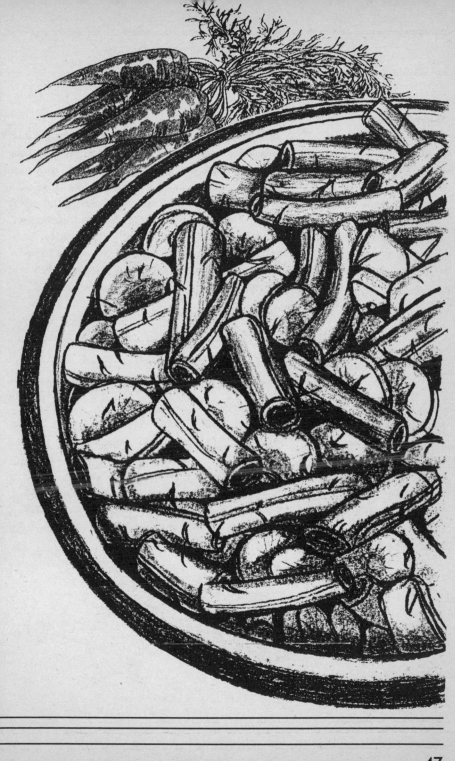

GREEN BEANS SUPREME

Ingredients:

2 cups water
1 pound green beans, ends removed
Salt to taste
3 tablespoons butter or margine
1/2 cup heavy cream
1/2 cup Parmesan cheese, grated

Directions:

Boil water in saucepan. Add green beans and salt. Let water come to boil once again. Reduce heat to medium-low and cook 15 minutes. Drain. Lightly coat bottom of baking dish with 1 tablespoon butter or margarine. Add green beans, remaining butter or margarine, cream and grated cheese. Toss gently until mixed well. Place in a 325°F oven and bake 10 minutes or until heated thoroughly. Do not allow cream to boil or it may curdle.

Serves: 4

GRILLED EGGPLANT SLICES

Ingredients:

1 large eggplant, cut in 3/4 inch thick slices
1 cup grated mozzarella cheese
1/4 cup flour
1/4 cup oil
2 tablespoons butter

Directions:

Peel the eggplant and cut into slices. Dredge them lightly with flour, dot with butter, and brush with oil. Grill as you would a hamburger, turning once during the cooking. Sprinkle each slice with grated cheese just as you turn it. Brush again with oil after you turn them and season to taste.

Serves: 4

HERBED BROILED TOMATOES

Ingredients:
4 large tomatoes, cut in
halves
1/4 teaspoon basil
1/4 teaspoon thyme
1/4 teaspoon tarragon
Salt to taste

Directions:
Arrange tomato halves in baking pan lined with foil. Combine basil, thyme, tarragon and salt. Mix well. Sprinkle evenly over tomatoes. Place in broiler 15 minutes or until skin of tomato is tender. *Options:* Sprinkle tomato with grated Parmesan cheese or shredded mozzarella cheese a few minutes before tomatoes are finished cooking. Add or substitute oregano, garlic or any of your favorite herbs and spices. *Helpful Hints:* Test doneness by piercing skin of tomato with fork. Fork should enter easily. Serve with any of your favorite meat, poultry or fish recipes.

Serves: 4 to 8

HONEY GLAZED CARROTS

Ingredients:
2 quarts water
Salt to taste
1 pound carrots, sliced
1/4 cup butter, melted
1/4 cup honey
1/4 cup raisins

Directions:
Boil water and add salt. Add carrots and cook 15 minutes or until tender. Drain. Stir in remaining ingredients.

Serves: 4 to 6

LEMON BRUSSELS SPROUTS

Ingredients:
2 quarts of water
2 teaspoons salt
1 pound fresh Brussels
sprouts
1/2 lemon

Directions:
Boil water and salt. Add Brussels sprouts. Cook, covered, over medium-low heat for 15 minutes. Drain. Remove to platter. Squeeze lemon over Brussels sprouts.

Serves: 4

LEMON-BUTTERED BROCCOLI

Ingredients:
1 cup water
1 bunch broccoli, ends
trimmed
Salt to taste
3 tablespoons butter,
melted
1 1/2 tablespoons
lemon juice

Directions:
Carefully break broccoli apart into spears. Boil water in large pot. Add broccoli and salt. Let water come to boil once again. Reduce heat to low, cover and steam 15 minutes. Broccoli should be tender, but still firm. Combine butter with lemon juice in small saucepan and heat, stirring constantly. Remove · broccoli from pot to serving platter. Pour lemon-butter sauce over top and serve. *Options:* Frozen broccoli spears can be substituted if fresh is out of season. Pour cheese sauce or white sauce over broccoli for a change of pace. *Helpful Hints:* Choose broccoli that is consistantly bright green in color. Yellow blemishes mean broccoli is over-ripe. Outer layer of larger stems are tough. Remove this outer layer with vegetable peeler. Do not overcook! This will result in colorless, wilted broccoli plus vitamins will be highly reduced!

Serves: 4

ITALIAN STYLE BEANS

Ingredients:
1 quart water
1 pound Italian green
  beans, ends removed
1/2 cup tomato sauce
2 tablespoons Parmesan
  cheese

Directions:
Place water and beans in saucepan. Bring to boil, reduce heat and cover. Simmer 20 minutes or until tender. Drain and stir in sauce. Heat thoroughly. Sprinkle with cheese. *Options:* Use canned tomatoes, drained, in place of sauce. Mushrooms are a delightful addition in this recipe. Frozen green beans can be substituted for fresh. *Helpful Hints:* Fresh beans should be dark green in color, without discoloration. Serve with any meat, poultry or seafood meal you plan.

Serves: 2 to 4

ITALIAN STYLE SPINACH

Ingredients:
2 8-ounces packages
  spinach, frozen,
  chopped
Salt to taste
2 cups water
2 tablespoons butter or
  margarine
1 tablespoon olive oil
1 teaspoon garlic
  powder
2 tablespoons Parmesan
  cheese, grated

Directions:
Place spinach and salt into boiling water. Reduce heat, cover and simmer 15 minutes or until just tender. Remove lid now and then, separating spinach with fork, as it thaws. Drain well and return to saucepan. Add butter, olive oil, and garlic. Stir, cover and simmer 2 minutes. Remove to serving dish and sprinkle with cheese. *Options:* Fresh or canned spinach can also be used with this recipe. *Helpful Hints:* This recipe is a great side dish with pasta.

Serves: 4

MINT GLAZED CARROTS

Ingredients:
1 quart water
3 carrots, sliced
1/2 cup butter or margarine
1/2 cup sugar
1 tablespoon mint leaves
2 cups peas, frozen
2 tablespoon butter or margarine
Salt and pepper to taste

Directions:
Boil water with salt. Add carrots. Cook 12 minutes or until tender. Drain. Stir in butter or margarine, sugar and mint. Cook over medium heat 8 minutes. Stir in peas. Heat through. Remove to platter. Stir in butter or margarine, salt and pepper.

Serves: 4 to 6

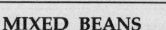

MIXED BEANS

Ingredients:
1 quart water
1/2 pound green beans, ends removed
1/2 pound wax beans, ends removed
3 strips bacon, chopped
Salt and pepper to taste

Directions:
Place water in saucepan. Slice beans into 1 1/2-inch pieces. Add beans and bacon to water. Bring to boil, reduce heat and cover. Simmer 20 minutes or until tender. Drain. Season with salt and pepper. *Options:* Add butter or margarine to cooked beans. Serve with slivered almonds for "Mixed Green Beans Almondine." *Helpful Hints:* Choose beans that are dark green and bright yellow without any discoloration. Fresh green beans will snap sharply when broken. Beans are a colorful side-dish for meat, poultry, or seafood platters.

Serves: 2 to 4

MUSHROOM SCALLOPED POTATOES

Ingredients:

1 tablespoon butter or margarine
4 cups potatoes, sliced
1 (10 1/2 ounce) can cream of mushroom soup, condensed
1/2 cup milk
Salt and pepper to taste
2 tablespoons bread crumbs, seasoned

Directions:

Coat baking dish with butter or margarine. Add potatoes. Combined soup, milk, salt and pepper. Pour over potatoes. Cover and bake in a 350°F oven 45 minutes. Sprinkle bread crumbs over top. Return to oven 15 minutes longer or until potatoes are tender. *Options:* Cream of celery soup can be used, if desired. Place thin layers of shredded Cheddar cheese between potatoes before pouring soup mixture over top.

Serves: 6

OKRA AND TOMATOES

Ingredients:

1/2 pound okra
2 cups tomatoes
1 clove garlic
Salt and pepper to taste

Directions:

Wash and trim okra stems. Place in saucepan. Add tomatoes, garlic, salt and pepper. Simmer 15 minutes or until desired tenderness is reached.

Serves: 2 to 4

POTATOES WITH BACON AND CHEESE

Ingredients:
3 large baking potatoes, pared and sliced
6 sliced, cooked bacon strips, crisp
1 large onion, thickly sliced
1/2 pound sharp processed American cheese, cubed
1/2 cup butter or margarine

Directions:
Arrange sliced potatoes on large piece of foil, and sprinkle with salt and pepper. Crumble bacon over top. Add onion and cheese cubes. Slice butter over all the potatoes. Bring edges of foil up keeping a very tiny hole open for expansion of steam. Seal sides well. Place package on grill. Cook over coals about 1 hour or until done. Move carefully on grill to heat evenly.

Serves: 6

RICE SOUFFLÉ

Ingredients:
2 quarts boiling water
1 tablespoon salt (if desired)
1 cup uncooked rice
4 eggs, separated
3/4 cups granulated sugar
4 cups milk
1/2 cup raisins (more if desired)
1/2 teaspoon ground cinnamon

Directions:
Put salt into boiling water. Add the rice slowly so boiling will not stop. Cook without stirring for 20 to 25 minutes or until tender. Drain. Beat the egg yolks and mix in the sugar and milk. Stir in the raisins and cinnamon. Beat the egg whites until peaks are formed. Fold into the rice mixture. Pour into a buttered 2-quart baking dish. Bake at 325°F for about 50 minutes.

Serves: 4

RED BEETS ITALIAN STYLE

Ingredients:
1 can beets, sliced, drained
1 clove garlic, crushed
2 tablespoons vinegar

Directions:
Stir all ingredients together. Cover and chill in refrigerator for 30 minutes.

Serves: 4

SAUTÉED BRUSSELS SPROUTS

Ingredients:
1 pound Brussels sprouts, stems and outer leaves removed
2 cups water
1/4 cup butter or margarine
Salt and pepper to taste

Directions:
Place Brussels sprouts in water. Bring to boil, reduce heat to medium-low and cover. Simmer 15 minutes or until tender but not soft. Drain and set aside. Melt butter or margarine in skillet. Slice Brussels sprouts in half through stems. Add to skillet, add salt and pepper to taste, and sauté 5 minutes, stirring often. *Options.* Sprinkle with grated cheese. Use drained whole tomatoes in place of butter or margarine. Brussels sprouts can be whole while sautéing, if desired. Pour cream sauce over top while sautéing. *Helpful Hints:* Slicing Brussels sprouts in half allows butter or margarine to be absorbed more thoroughly.

Serves: 4

SAUTÉED SUMMER ZUCCHINI

Ingredients:
1/4 cup butter or
  margarine
1 clove garlic, minced
2 cups zucchini, sliced
Salt and pepper to taste

Directions:
Melt butter or margarine in skillet. Add garlic. Sauté 2 minutes. Add zucchini, salt and pepper. Sauté over low heat for 20 minutes. Stir now and then.

Serves: 2 to 4

SAVORY STUFFED MUSHROOMS

Ingredients:
12 large mushrooms,
  whole
4 tablespoons
  mushroom stems,
  from whole
  mushrooms, chopped
4 tablespoons bread
  crumbs
4 tablespoons Parmesan
  cheese, grated
2 teaspoons butter or
  margarine
1 1/2 cups tomato
  sauce

Directions:
Separate stems from caps of mushrooms. Chop enough stems to make 4 tablespoons. Combine stems with bread crumbs, cheese and butter or margarine, in saucepan. Warm slowly, over low heat, until butter or margarine melts. Mix thoroughly. Stuff each mushroom cap with mixture. Arrange in baking dish. Pour sauce over top. Cover with foil and bake in a 375°F oven for 30 minutes or until mushrooms are tender. *Options:* Add finely chopped onion, if desired.

Serves: 6

SCALLOPED POTATOES

Ingredients:

5 potatoes, peeled,
  sliced thin
2 medium onions, sliced
Salt to taste
2 quarts water
1/2 cup milk
2 tablespoons flour
2 tablespoons cheese,
  Parmesan, grated

Directions:

Boil potatoes and onions in salted water until potatoes are half cooked. Drain and set aside. In saucepan, add milk and flour. Stir until smooth. Heat 5 minutes or until hot and bubbly. Pour both potatoes and milk mixture in shallow casserole dish. Sprinkle cheese over top. Place in a 350°F oven for 35 minutes or until golden brown.

Serves: 4

STIR-FRIED SPINACH

Ingredients:
2 tablespoons peanut oil
1 pound spinach, chopped
1/4 cup water chestnuts
2 tablespoons soy sauce
Salt and pepper to taste

Directions:
Heat cooking oil in large skillet until hot. Add spinach and water chestnuts. Stir-fry by constantly stirring spinach over medium-high heat for 1 minute. Remove from skillet to platter. Sprinkle with soy sauce, salt and pepper. *Options:* Sesame seed oil can be used in place of peanut oil. Garlic or ginger add flavor. Use a Chinese wok. They are ideal for stir-frying. Add slivered almonds, if desired. *Helpful Hints:* While stir-frying, stir constantly to prevent scorching.

Serves: 4

STUFFED ARTICHOKES

Ingredients:
4 to 6 artichokes
1 can seasoned bread crumbs

Directions:
Cut off bottoms and tops of artichokes and snip each tip. Wash and then stuff each leaf with bread crumbs. Use 1 tablespoon of oil to moisten bread crumbs before filling artichokes. Turn artichokes upside down and pat gently to remove excess bread crumbs. Place artichokes in a large pot with 1 inch of water and as soon as water comes to a boil, turn heat to low and simmer approximately 1 hour. When artichokes turn dark green in color, they are done.

Serves: 4 to 6

SPECIAL STUFFED POTATOES

Ingredients:
4 medium baking potatoes
1/2 cup green pepper, diced
1/4 cup butter or margarine
1/2 cup hot milk
1 teaspoon salt
1/2 teaspoon ground pepper
1/4 cup sour cream

Directions:
Wrap each potato in foil and bake at 400°F for 1 hour or until baked all the way through. Slice one side of each potato lengthwise and scoop out the middle completely. Set potato skin aside. Sauté green pepper in 1 tablespoon butter or margarine until tender. Remove from heat. Mash scooped out center of potato with milk, remaining butter or margarine, salt and pepper. Stir in green peppers and sour cream. Mix well. Refill potato skins with mixture. Bake at 325°F for 15 minutes.

Serves: 4

INDEX

Vegetables